THEMES IN RELIGI

HINDUISM

S.C. Mercier

SERIES EDITOR: CLIVE ERRICKER
Lecturer in Arts Education
University of Warwick

About the Themes in Religion series

This series of books offers a lively and accessible introduction to the six main world religions for students taking GCSE Religious Studies. The books can be used separately to study one religious tradition, or they can be used together, to investigate one theme across the traditions, such as beliefs, worship, pilgrimage or values. The section on values shows how each religion reacts to everyday life and the modern world. The spreads offer class activities and assignments that relate to coursework requirements and encourage further research, and each book provides a glossary of important terms and a reading list.

Each spread is self-contained and presents an important aspect of each religion. Through carefully chosen photographs, clear text and relevant quotations from scriptures and believers, students will learn about each religion and the living impact it has for believers today. The wide variety of assignments help pupils to evaluate what they have read, suggest activities to further their understanding, and raise issues for them to reflect on.

We hope that these books will provide students of all abilities with a stimulating introduction to these religions, and that the enjoyment of using them matches that of producing them.

Clive Erricker

About Hinduism

The richness and variety of Hinduism makes it a valuable religion for study at GCSE. Hinduism offers the student an ideal opportunity for looking at diversity within religious belief and practice. This in turn can help the student to develop important skills and attitudes: open-mindedness, the capacity to feel at home with rather than be intimidated by diversity, and the ability to recognise continuity as well as difference and change.

This book has no separate section on the Hindu scriptures. This is because Hinduism is not a 'religion of the book' in the way some religions are said to be. However, there are frequent references to and quotations from the key scriptures in the text, and through these students will build up a general knowledge and understanding of the place and importance of scriptures in Hindu belief and practice.

S.C. Mercier

Thank You
I would like to thank V.P. (Hemant) Kanitkar; members of the Gujurati Centre, Preston; and members of the Indian Community Centre, Reading for their help.

CONTENTS

WORSHIP
Worshipping God	4
Image, shrine and temple	6
Worship in the home	8
God within	10
An Arti service	12

BELIEFS AND CONCEPTS
Is there a God?	14
Life cycles	16
Paths to freedom	18
Class and caste	20
Dharma	22

RITES OF PASSAGE
Childhood celebrations	24
Stages in life	26
The sacred thread	28
A wedding	30
Cremation	32

CELEBRATIONS
Shiva Ratri	34
Spring festivals	36
Janamashtami	38
Nava Ratri	40
Diwali	42

PILGRIMAGE
An act of devotion	44
The river Ganges	46
Guru as God	48
Personal pilgrimage	50

VALUES
The world	52
Non-violence	54
War and peace	56
Love and marriage	58
Community service	60

Glossary	62
Index	63
Further reading	64

WORSHIP

WORSHIPPING GOD

- How would you express the following in actions without words:
  a) saying thank you?
  b) saying sorry?
  c) showing respect to someone important?
  d) showing love or friendship?
  How might these things be expressed in worship? Work out your ideas in groups. Discuss them in class.

What is worship?

- Look at the expression and gesture of the boy in the photo. List clues that tell you that he is at worship. What do you think he is thinking? In pairs discuss questions you would have to ask to find out.

> 'We like to show our love and respect for God not only in words but with our whole selves, and in actions and gestures. We feel God is present when we open our hearts to him, and so we honour him as we would show reverence to an honoured guest.'

Hinduism is a very ancient religion going back to about 2,000 BCE. It grew up in the vast Indian subcontinent, and so worship often varies from one community to another. God is worshipped in different forms and in different ways, but the Hindu scriptures say this is acceptable. The best known of the scriptures is the **Bhagavad Gita**, which means 'The Song of the Lord'. In this, God appears in the form of the Lord **Krishna**. He said:

> Even those who worship other gods with love
> And sacrifice to them, full filled with faith,
> Do really worship me.

Hindus say that God is One. They believe there is One Supreme Spirit of the universe called **Brahman**. Many Hindus call this God. Brahman they say is in all things. Brahman is present and can be worshipped in the highest mountain and in the smallest seed. This Supreme Spirit dwells in every living creature and is the soul of every being.

How do Hindus worship?

Hindu worship can be expressed in words or offerings, in song and dance, or simply in silent devotion. Worship can be full of ceremony and ritual, or be very simple, as Krishna said:

> Be it a leaf, or flower, or fruit, or water
> That a zealous soul may offer with love's devotion
> That do I willingly accept,
> For it was love that made the offering.

ASSIGNMENTS

- Discuss the meaning of Krishna's teachings with a partner.
- Imagine one of you is the worshipper in the photo and you want to explain to a friend how you express your devotion to God. Work out your conversation in questions and answers. Say how different forms of worship are acceptable to God according to the teachings of Hinduism. Act out your role-play in class.

KEY WORDS

Bhagavad Gita Krishna
Brahman

Worshipping Krishna in a Hindu temple in Britain

WORSHIP

IMAGE, SHRINE AND TEMPLE

● With a partner discuss how you might draw or represent people with the following powers using pictures or symbols:
a) the power to see all things
b) the power to protect or save
c) the power to destroy evil
d) the power to provide the needs of the world.

Images of God

Many people have a picture in their mind of what God is like. Hindus use images – statues and pictures – in their worship. An image is like the photo of a loved one. A photo may be treasured and be a reminder of someone but it cannot take the place of the person. In Hindu worship the image cannot stand in the place of God, it is simply a symbol for devotion.

● What pictures of God do people have in their minds? List some of the words and names you have heard people use when talking about God e.g. King, Lord. Share your ideas with a friend. Discuss why you think people find these images useful.

A house for God

Most villages in India have a shrine which houses a local god or goddess. The villagers care for the image and make daily offerings. In the larger villages and towns there are temples. A temple is a house for a god. Since the gods were once thought to live in the Himalayas, many temples reflect the shapes of mountains. At the heart of the temple is a cave-like chamber containing the image. Approaching the image is a reminder of the inward journey a person must make into the depths of their heart when they approach God.

● Compare the photo with the one on page 5. Identify and discuss similarities and differences with a partner.

> 'When we go to worship at the temple we must first take a bath and put on clean clothes. We must also make sure we are not impure in our minds and hearts. So we make sure that we do not carry thoughts of hatred or envy but only offerings of love when we go to pray.'

Worshippers visit the deity at the temple in much the same way as they might drop in on a well-loved friend. They may take a gift such as fresh flowers or food to offer at the shrine. At the temple the priest looks after the images and performs the daily rituals, reciting verses from the holy scriptures. The worshippers watch and listen. They may pray or chant a **mantra** repeating the god's name. On festive occasions people gather at the temple to sing devotional hymns called **bhajans**.

WORSHIP 7

ASSIGNMENTS

● Imagine you are a worshipper visiting the temple. Describe how you prepare for worship. Explain what you see, hear and do when you are there. Explain how your visit is an expression of love and how there are other ways to express this devotion. Say which way you prefer and say why. Use other books on Hinduism to help you.

KEY WORDS

mantra   bhajan

A Hindu temple in India

8 WORSHIP

WORSHIP IN THE HOME

● How does the day begin in your home? How does it compare with the Hindu household described in the quotation opposite? Share your answers with a friend.

A Hindu family shrine in a house in London

WORSHIP

> 'My mother gets up first, when it is still dark. She bathes and gets dressed and then prays at the shrine. She bathes the god and puts incense and offerings of flowers and food in front of it. Then she lights the ghee lamp and says a prayer. After that she prepares the breakfast, wakes us and gets ready for work.'

> May the eternal light of the Creator Enlighten and purify our minds and hearts.

There are many different translations and interpretations of this mantra (see also page 25).

Family prayer

Most Hindus worship at a shrine at home. It contains a picture or a small statue of a god and every morning the deity is 'awakened' with light, food and prayers. These acts of devotion are called **puja**.

● Look at the photo. With a friend find six things you can identify as important in Hindu worship.

Some families worship together at the shrine. The deity is offered refreshment and treated as an honoured guest. **Panchamrit** is made to bathe the image. This is a mixture of yogurt, honey, milk, ghee (clarified butter) and sugar. The image is dressed, adorned with flowers and anointed with sandalwood paste, turmeric and red kumkum powder. Incense is burned and a bell summons and proclaims the presence of the deity. A ghee lamp is lit and moved in a circle before the face of the god. This offering of light is called **Arti**. Everyone receives the light, passing their hands over the flame and lifting them across the face and hair. The **Gayatri Mantra** is recited daily by most Hindus.

Blessed food

At mealtimes a portion of food is offered at the shrine. It is returned to the table and the food becomes **parshad**, blessed food. Sweets and cakes offered to the gods are shared out so that the children learn to give thanks for God's blessings.

● Set up a shrine in class. Draw and label each item. With a friend work out how each of these things appeals to the senses and involves the worshipper. Say why you think puja is the way most Hindus like to worship and what problems might arise with this form of worship. Jot down ideas and share them in class.

ASSIGNMENTS

● Imagine you belong to the family of the girl in the photo. Your teacher asks you to explain worship in your home. Prepare a talk for your class. Say why family worship means a lot to you.

KEY WORDS

puja   panchamrit   Arti
Gayatri Mantra   parshad

GOD WITHIN

The oldest Hindu scriptures are the **Vedas**. They contain hymns and prayers to the gods. Attached to the Vedas are the **Upanishads**. This word means 'to sit down near', as a student sits by a teacher. The Upanishads contain teachings of the holy men of ancient India who pondered the nature of Brahman. Some Hindus today spend many hours in meditation and devote their lives in search of true knowledge of Brahman. Someone who follows this path is called a **sannyasin**.

A yantra

WORSHIP

- Jot down words to describe how your mind feels, e.g. sluggish, busy, like a butterfly. Does the feeling alter with your mood? Write down what you think. Share your thoughts in class.
- In silence focus your mind on the yantra on page 10 for a few minutes. In pairs discuss how this concentration felt to you.
- Many Hindus meditate for a time each day. Could starting the day with a few minutes quietness and calm be helpful? Try this for a few days, report back in class and write up your conclusions.

Learning to meditate

The sannyasin must learn self-discipline and live a life of truthfulness, unselfishness and gentleness towards other beings. He gives up all possessions and physical distractions. However, thoughts and feelings distract too. So the sannyasin learns to meditate. There are many ways to meditate. A **yantra** can be used to focus the mind and prevent thoughts from wandering. Sacred mantras also help concentration. For example, the sacred sound and symbol **OM** may be recited as a chant. It represents Eternal Truth. Yoga is also used to help to control the body and the senses so that the mind can be calm and free from distractions. (Yoga means 'yoke' or self-discipline and refers to an ancient system of exercises to discipline the body and the senses.)

The sacred symbol OM

Losing oneself

The path of meditation is not worship in the usual sense. The aim of the sannyasin is to lose himself and to become one with Brahman:

> 'As rivers flowing downwards find their home
> In the ocean, leaving name and form behind,
> So does the man who knows, from name and form released,
> Draw near to the divine Person who is beyond the beyond.'
>
> [Chandogya Upanishad VI, x, 1]

ASSIGNMENTS

- Find out more about the following: a) mantras b) yantras c) yoga. Write a short explanation of each and give an example or illustration. Check your notes with a friend to see if they are clear.

KEY WORDS

Vedas   Upanishads   sannyasin
yantra   OM

AN ARTI SERVICE

Many Hindu temples in Britain are converted churches or halls, and they are often called **mandirs**. The mandir may be a cultural centre as well as a place for worship. The priest there performs daily puja and presides over family celebrations such as weddings.

Many mandirs in Britain have a regular Arti service. As people enter the shrine room they remove their shoes. This is both a sign of respect and very practical. They approach the shrines, bow and make a small offering of food or money. The service begins with the singing of bhajans, often accompanied on the harmonium. The priest prepares a tray with a ghee lamp, a fan, a shell, offerings of water, rice, food, incense, flowers and a small bell. With this he approaches the gods and performs puja, reciting verses from the scriptures.

Receiving the light

The climax of the ceremony is when the priest lifts the lamp to each deity, moving it in a circle. At the same time he rings a small bell to summon the deity. The singing and clapping gets louder. Finally the priest faces the congregation and circles the lamp once again.

Sometimes the Arti lamp is taken around the congregation and everyone receives the light by passing their hands over the flame and then over the face and hair.

The service ends with everyone sharing parshad, the food that has been offered and blessed.

- Receiving the light and sharing parshad are important symbolic actions. Discuss their meaning with a partner.

> Through the ritual of Arti the presence of God comes alive in the images ... and in the hearts of the worshippers ... we must keep the love of God alight in our hearts to purify and enlighten us.

ASSIGNMENTS

- Imagine you are an RE teacher preparing a class visit to a mandir.
  a) Make a list of things you would want your class to find out.
  b) Write a set of questions for them.
  c) List the vocabulary you want pupils to know.
  d) Put down the questions you would want to ask the priest at the mandir yourself.
  Share your ideas with a partner.

- Plan a new Hindu temple and community centre showing the shrine room and necessary facilities.
  a) Design and write an illustrated leaflet to advertise worship and activities at the mandir (use the photo right and the sample timetable on page 61 to help you).
  b) Write about the value of the mandir for the life of the Hindu community as if you were the chairman of the mandir committee encouraging the people to come along.

WORSHIP 13

- Write a talk on Hindu worship. (You could use some other books on Hinduism to help you.) Explain what happens and how the use of symbols and activities are encouraged in order to help the worshipper. Say how helpful you think images, music, mantras and other aids to worship are and point out some of the possible pitfalls the devotee needs to be aware of.

KEY WORDS

mandir

Performing Arti at a temple

BELIEFS AND CON...

IS THERE A GOD?

Shiva, whose mighty powers are controlled through asceticism and meditation

If we ask 'Is there a God?' and look at what Hinduism has to say, we find different answers. Some Hindus say there is no God, only Brahman. Brahman is the Supreme Spirit of the universe. Brahman is not usually described as a person but as Spirit or the Infinite:

> 'This Infinite is below, it is above, it is to the west, to the east, to the south, to the north. Truly it is this whole universe.'
>
> [Chandogya Upanishad VII, xxv]

- There are no pictures or images to represent Brahman. Brahman is even difficult to put into words. Discuss why this is. Try to capture the Hindu view of Brahman in your own words, in a poem or prayer or story or even in a picture.

One God but many names

Some Hindu scriptures say that Brahman can be known in the form of God. God is known by many names. One of the best known is **Shiva**, the Supreme Lord.

- Look at the photo and list words and phrases which describe the kind of God which is being portrayed in this image.

The scriptures also say that God can be seen as a personal God who can be known as a friend. He is then called Lord **Vishnu**. Vishnu appears on earth in different forms to save the world. He is best loved in the forms of Rama and Krishna. Some Hindus worship God in the female form. She is known as Amba or Durga or Kali. People talk about God in different ways but really God is too great to grasp, like the elephant in this famous Hindu story:

> There was once a blind man who wanted to know what an elephant was. So people brought one for him to touch. The man put out his hand and felt the trunk and said it was like a tree. His companions were also blind and wanted to find out about this creature. One grasped the ear and said it was like a fan. Another took hold of the tail and said it was like a rope. So each one believed he had the answer but none of them had grasped the whole truth.

- How does the story of the blind men help us to understand that there are different ways of talking about God? Discuss this in class. Compose your own story to give a similar teaching.

ASSIGNMENTS

- Find out more about: a) Brahman b) Shiva c) Vishnu.
- Plan an imaginary interview with three Hindus to discuss their ideas of God. Write questions and answers to show at least three different views and explain why it might be helpful to think of God in all these ways. In your conclusion say which view of God you think is the most helpful and explain why.

KEY WORDS

Shiva   Vishnu

LIFE CYCLES

Every action has an effect. Everything that happens has a cause. Hindus call this the law of **karma**. Karma means actions.

This is your life

In the scriptures called the Upanishads are teachings of the holy men of ancient India. These wise men discussed the nature of the human soul. The Hindu word for soul is **atman**. Some said that atman is really the same spirit as Brahman and therefore eternal. They then asked: How does the soul get trapped in a body which dies? The answer seemed to be because of 'karma'.

People do not realise their true nature is Brahman. They try to find happiness by satisfying the body and its desires. But the things of this world cannot satisfy the soul whose true nature is spirit. Striving for happiness in physical things only leads to karma, which binds the soul to this physical existence.

Life after life

Hindus believe that when the body dies the soul lives on. It takes on a new life in another body. But the karma from previous lives leaves an impression which is carried over. Evil or selfish actions carve out an unhappy future. Unselfish action brings benefits in the next life. So the soul continues through life after life. This is reincarnation. Hindus call this continually reincarnated existence **samsara**. In the Bhagavad Gita it is described in this way:

> As a man casts off his worn-out clothes
> And takes on other new ones in their place,
> So does the embodied soul cast off his worn-out bodies
> And enters others new.
>
> [Bhagavad Gita II, 22]

Caught up in the eternal wheel of karma and samsara the soul cannot be free.

● Draw a diagram to show the eternal wheel of life, death and rebirth, i.e. the cycle of samsara. Beside it write a commentary explaining how it works and what it represents for somebody looking at these ideas for the first time.

> 'You have lived many many lives. Why? Because everything you do attaches you to this worldly existence. Be free from desire, hatred, greed and envy. Act, but do not be attached to the outcome of your actions. Then you will be free from the effects of karma. Then you will be free from samsara.'

BELIEFS AND CONCEPTS 17

ASSIGNMENTS

- Look at the photo. Imagine you are visiting India and have heard this guru's teaching on karma and samsara. Write a letter home telling people what he said. Say how this teaching would affect you if you believed it to be the truth about life. Say what makes you have doubts about it and what appeals to you about the theory of karma and samsara.

KEY WORDS

karma   atman   samsara

A Hindu guru preaching

BELIEFS AND CONCEPTS

PATHS TO FREEDOM

What is real?

● Draw yourself at the centre of a page. Around you list the people and possessions you are attached to. Look at the picture with a friend and discuss whether these attachments are good or whether they could become a burden.

Hinduism teaches that the things of this world are like reflections on the surface of reality. The world is maya, or appearance only, and things which seem important in this life are like dreams that offer no lasting happiness. That which is real,

BELIEFS AND CONCEPTS

lasting and life-giving is unseen. That is Brahman.

● Sometimes we feel tied down by worries or pain or just daily routine. We may long to be free from all these things. Write a poem or prayer expressing the longing to be free.

> From the unreal lead me to the real!
> From darkness lead me to the light!
> From death lead me to immortality!
>
> [Brihadaranyaka Upanishad I, iii, 28]

This prayer is from the Upanishads. They contain teachings about how to free the soul from the endless cycle of samsara. The word for this freedom is **moksha**. Moksha is described in many ways, such as 'perfect peace' or 'happiness'. Sometimes it is described as the soul losing itself in Brahman, like a grain of salt dissolved in water. At other times it is said to be the joy or bliss of union with God.

Three paths

Every desire, every attachment, every thought of self binds the soul to the chain of rebirth. For the soul to be free, these chains must be broken. There are several paths to moksha. There is **jnana yoga**, the way of knowledge. Through meditation it is possible to know the truth and let go the attachments of this world so that the chains of karma fall away and moksha is reached.

There is the path of unselfish action, or **karma yoga**. By doing one's daily work without grudge, and free from the desire for selfish gain, it is possible to live unattached to this world. Then the bonds of karma fall away bringing perfect peace.

The path followed by most Hindus is **bhakti yoga**, the way of devotion. This can find expression in daily worship, in prayer and offerings. The women in the photo are expressing their love for Krishna in dance. The path of bhakti is God-centred rather than self-centred, so the chains of attachment are loosened. Then nothing stands in the way of the soul's union with God.

ASSIGNMENTS

● Use symbols or pictures and words to describe different paths to moksha. Say which path you think would be the suitable one for most people to follow, or suggest which combination of paths would be best, and explain why. Also explain which path you think *you* would find most suitable. You may wish to research further before doing this task.

● Hindu teaching says there are three strands or 'gunas' which influence the way we feel and what we do. Sattva is the strand related to goodness and truth. Tamas is to do with darkness and heaviness. The Rajas guna is light and energy and passion. Look back over the last twenty-four hours and try to work out how such gunas might be said to have been at work in your activities, your moods and feelings. Share your thoughts with a friend. Discuss what you think of this theory of the three gunas.

KEY WORDS

moksha   jnana yoga   karma yoga
bhakti yoga

CLASS AND CASTE

The four varnas

● Look at the way in which your school and class is divided into groups. Which divisions are helpful and which are unhelpful? Discuss these questions in pairs and share your ideas in class.

In the sacred Vedas there is a myth about how society came to be divided up in ancient India. It tells of Primal Man, a huge giant, who was sacrificed. His mouth became the priests, or **brahmins**. His arms became the princes and warriors, called **kshatriyas**. His thighs were the merchants, or **vaishyas**. His feet became the **shudra**, or servants. These were the four **varnas**. They were used to represent the divisions of society in India.

● Represent the four varnas of ancient Hindu society in a picture/diagram, using the story from the Vedas to help you.

Another group of people appeared. They were known as 'outcastes'. Because their work was considered unclean or contaminating, they were called 'untouchables'. Discrimination against untouchables is now illegal but the prejudice remains.

Jati

As communities grew and developed, Hindu society became divided up according to trades and professions. Everyone was born into a particular group depending on the work or background of their parents. This social grouping became known as **jati**, or caste groups. Marriage and other social contacts were kept within the same caste. These divisions can especially be seen in village India and still exist in the towns and cities, but for Hindus living in Britain the divisions are no longer as important.

The Laws of Manu

According to Hindu scriptures, such as the Laws of Manu, everyone has a duty in life. This duty is called 'dharma'. The dharma of those in power was to ensure peace and stability. Those in business were to work hard to bring prosperity. Those who served others were to do so honestly and ungrudgingly. Priests and teachers had a duty to ensure the spiritual well-being of the people. Today most Hindus believe that their dharma is to worship God, to perform their daily duty to the best of their ability and to work for the benefit of the community.

A priest explains his duties:

> 'The scriptures set out important rituals which I follow when preparing and looking after the temple images.

BELIEFS AND CONCEPTS 21

Worshippers bring offerings and come to listen to the teachings of the scriptures. As the priest, I am responsible for attending to shrines and performing puja. Sometimes I am asked to preside over a wedding ceremony or to recite prayers when someone dies.

ASSIGNMENTS

● Look at the priest in the photo. Prepare a set of questions you could ask a Hindu priest about his duty or dharma. Write an interview with him in which he explains how he understands his work. Write an interview with a worshipper at the temple too, who says how and why he or she values the work of the priest. Say what you think the value of the work of the priest is in the temple and community. You could use some other books on Hinduism to help you with this.

KEY WORDS

brahmin   kshatriya   vaishya
shudra   varna   jati

A priest performing his duties at the temple

DHARMA

● Discuss the duties of the following: a) a father b) a teacher c) a prime minister d) a husband e) a wife f) a son or daughter.

Rama enthroned as God and king with his wife Sita at his side

The word **dharma** is important in Hinduism. It means 'what is right'. It refers to the laws governing the duties of people and the laws governing the universe. Dharma can mean law or duty or even 'religion'. It has both a moral and a

BELIEFS AND CONCEPTS

religious meaning. Hindus call their religion **Sanatandharma** or Eternal Dharma.

● With a partner discuss the meaning of the words a) duty, b) religion. Share your ideas in class.

There are many Hindu texts with teachings on dharma. One of the best loved is the poem called the Ramayana, the story of **Rama**.

Prince Rama

Prince Rama was a virtuous and obedient son and rightful heir to the throne. However, Rama's father had once promised his second wife two wishes and when the king was old she demanded that her own son be made king and Rama be sent into exile for fourteen years. The old king kept his promise but died broken-hearted. All the people wanted Rama as their king and even the queen's son refused to take the throne. Nevertheless, Rama knew it was his duty to honour his father's word. So he and his wife, Princess Sita, went into exile. During that time Rama conquered the powers of evil and destroyed the tyrant Ravana who had kidnapped Sita. Eventually Rama and Sita returned to their palace and were crowned. Rama established peace in his kingdom and ruled over his people with justice. He never put his own comfort before the good of his subjects and he fulfilled his true dharma as son, as prince, as warrior, as husband and eventually as king.

God made man

Hindus see Rama as the perfect man and as an example of obedience to dharma. The loyalty and love between Rama and Sita are a model for married couples. Rama is worshipped as an **avatar** of Vishnu. Avatar means God's 'down-coming' on earth.

● Look at the photo of Rama as an avatar of Vishnu. He is enthroned with his wife Sita. His faithful brother Laksmana, who went with him into exile, is at his side. Hanuman the monkey-god helped him find Sita and represents the true servant and perfect devotee. With a partner discuss how this image represents Rama. Try to put together words and phrases that a Hindu might use to describe Rama. Make your ideas into the words of a Hindu prayer or hymn.

ASSIGNMENTS

● Find out more about Rama's time in exile. Produce a book for Hindu children telling the story in words and pictures and reminding them of its religious teachings.

● Imagine you are a Hindu. You have moved into a new neighbourhood. Write an article for the local newspaper on your religion and call it 'Sanatandharma'. Explain what this means and, keeping in mind the difficulties the readers may have in understanding the way you live and worship, try to explain how your life is guided by a) the teachings and b) the practices of your religion. Use other books on Hinduism to help you.

KEY WORDS

dharma   Sanatandharma   Rama   avatar

RITES OF PASSAGE

CHILDHOOD CELEBRATIONS

- Join with a partner. Imagine you are parents of a young child. Write down what would be the most important and exciting stages or moments in the child's life and development for you.

In the Hindu home there are special times during the development of a child even before it is born. At about the fourth to sixth month of pregnancy there is a celebration for the mother-to-be. It is carried out in the home by the women of the family. A ritual fire is lit in a container and prayers and offerings are made to God. This fire ritual is called **Havan**. The expectant mother is garlanded with flowers and anointed with perfumed oils. Special foods are prepared to satisfy her longings and she is encouraged to taste every dish.

Birth

In the past the priest would have ritually washed the baby as a symbol of purification. Today the midwife or nurse washes it. However, the priest may still be invited to carry out a ritual cleansing shortly after the birth. He recites prayers and hymns from the scriptures and sprinkles the mother and baby with drops of water as a sign of purification.

Some families have a special ceremony when the father holds his child for the first time. The father dips a gold jewel into a mixture of ghee and honey and touches the lips of the baby with it. He asks God's protection for the child and whispers a prayer into its ear.

- With a partner discuss the hopes and fears a father may have in mind when he holds his child for the first time. Write a prayer the father might say on this occasion.

> 'We believe that birth is rebirth. The soul has lived before but it is being kindled in a new life on earth. So we pray that this life will be better than the previous life and we hope that we will lead the child to the knowledge of God.'

Naming the baby

The naming ceremony takes place twelve days after birth. The baby is dressed in new clothes. Traditionally it is placed in a swinging cot and twelve ghee lamps are lit around it. The priest announces the name chosen by the parents and recites prayers and hymns of praise. Afterwards there is a festive meal.

Other important occasions are also celebrated, for example the child's first haircut. The first time the child goes out is marked by a ceremony in which the father takes the baby into the sunshine and recites the sacred Gayatri Mantra:

> Let us meditate on the Divine Source of Light
> May it illuminate our thoughts and prayers.

A naming ceremony in Britain

ASSIGNMENTS

- Imagine you are a Hindu excited by the arrival of a baby brother or sister. Write to your grandmother in India about the occasions you have celebrated before and after the birth.
- Look at the Gayatri Mantra (see also page 9). What does the symbol of light represent on these occasions? Use the symbol to design an invitation to a naming ceremony. Inside or on the back of the invitation write a hymn or prayer that would be appropriate for such an occasion.

KEY WORDS

Havan

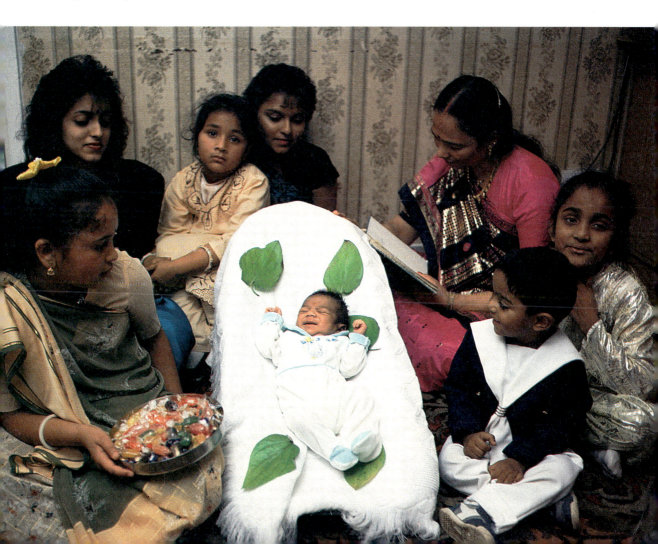

STAGES IN LIFE

● Look back at your life. Does it fall into a pattern or into stages? What stages do you see ahead of you? Which are you looking forward to? Write down your answers then discuss them with a partner.

Four stages

There are four stages in life according to Hindu teaching. These are called **ashrama** and they were set out for members of the brahmin, kshatriya and vaishya varnas of society. Each stage is defined by a particular dharma.

After childhood the first stage is called **brahma charya**, when the young person must take their education seriously and devote their time to their studies.

The second stage is the householder, called **grihastha**. It begins with marriage. This is when a person's energies are employed in running a home and bringing up a family or earning a living. It is the busiest time in a person's life, concerned with the duties to children, parents and husband or wife.

RITES OF PASSAGE

The third stage is **vanprasthashram**. It begins when the children have grown up and left home. Then it is time to turn from securing material well-being to spiritual well-being through prayer and studying the scriptures.

Preparing for death

The final stage is that of the sannyasin. It is the life of the recluse or world renouncer. Most people are still too occupied working or helping their children to completely renounce the world in their old age. Only a few Hindus take on the life of this stage. It means leaving behind familiar places and faces to live a life of meditation in the quest for moksha.

This is how a Hindu talked about the stages of life:

> 'When you are a student you must always try to be a good student. When you are a father you must try to be a good father ... when you've fulfilled your duties to your family, then you should devote the rest of your life to prayer and preparation for death.'

ASSIGNMENTS

● Draw and explain an illustrated 'map' of the Hindu stages of life.

● Look at the photo. How do you think each member of this Hindu family would see her or his dharma? Write your answer as a set of short interviews with three different members of the family. Show how these stages in life help people to understand their duty and purpose in life.

● Look back at what you wrote about your own life. Think about the ways in which your own pattern of life and that of the Hindu are different or similar. Write as thoughtfully as you can about why there are these similarities and differences. Before doing this task you may wish to research further in Hinduism.

KEY WORDS

ashrama   brahma charya
grihastha   vanprasthashram

Three generations of a Hindu family

28 | RITES OF PASSAGE

THE SACRED THREAD

RITES OF PASSAGE

Hinduism offers a sort of map or guide for the different stages in life. Each stage is marked by a sacred ritual or **samskar**.

● Look at the boy in the photo. In pairs list the clues that tell you this is an important occasion for him.

> 'I am now called "twice-born" because I have received the sacred thread. I suppose you could say it is a sort of spiritual birth. I must now concentrate more on spiritual matters and take my religion much more seriously.'

● What are the demands made on young people as they approach adolescence? What do they need as a sort of survival kit to go through growing up? With a partner draw up a list of skills, qualities and strengths of character you think a young person needs.

A time for study

In Hinduism there is a ceremony for some castes called the **Upanayam** or Sacred Thread Ceremony. It is for boys between the ages of eight and sixteen and marks the beginning of the student stage in life. In the past the boy left home to receive his education from a guru or spiritual teacher. He would have learnt meditation and the language and teachings of the Vedas. Today fewer boys undergo the ceremony and leave home in this way.

A boy at the Sacred Thread Ceremony in a temple in India

Receiving the thread

The ceremony is often held in the home around a ritual fire. The priest leads the ceremony, reciting from the scriptures. The boy and his father make offerings of ghee and incense and the father recites the Gayatri Mantra. His son repeats it and says that he will be guided by his teacher. He then makes a vow of celibacy (no sexual relations) and receives a white thread which rests on the left shoulder and hangs diagonally across the chest. It is made of three strands tied with a knot called the 'spiritual knot'. The priest promises to take the boy under his care as a son. Afterwards the boy's relatives celebrate the occasion with festive foods.

● Look at the photo:
  a) What might the white bag on the stick signify?
  b What is the meaning of the fire?

ASSIGNMENTS

● Imagine you are a young Hindu boy who has just received his sacred thread. It is bedtime and you write up this important day in your diary. Describe what happened and what the ceremony meant for you. Say how you felt at the time.

● How do you think that going through this ceremony may help a young Hindu boy growing up? Are there any ways in which it might make this period in life more difficult for him? Discuss your ideas in pairs then write them down in your own words.

KEY WORDS

samskar   Upanayam

30 RITES OF PASSAGE

A WEDDING

RITES OF PASSAGE

- If you get married, what do you want your wedding to be like? Why? Write down your ideas and share them with a friend. Discuss them in class.

The importance of marriage in the Hindu community is expressed in the samskar, or ritual, of the wedding. The ceremony differs from one community to another. In India it would take place at the bride's home. In Britain a hall may be booked for the occasion. The bride is dressed by sisters and female cousins and aunts. The sari and jewellery will be gifts from her family.

- Look at the photo. List all the things which point to the importance of this occasion. Compare your work with a friend.

The sacred fire

A priest leads the ceremony. He prepares for the Havan by lighting the ritual fire and reciting hymns calling on the gods to bless the occasion. When the groom arrives he is garlanded with flowers. The couple are seated by the sacred fire. In the past there would have been a veil between the couple until they were married as they would not have known each other. Today the couple will have met but often the bride and groom still partly cover their faces. The bride's father gives his daughter's right hand into the hand of her future husband. Sometimes the bride's brothers give her rice grains to pour into the groom's hands. It is a reminder that she will have to flourish and grow in a new home.

Seven steps

The priest recites verses from the scriptures in Sanskrit (the ancient language of the Vedas) and leads the couple through their meaning. The bride, her father and the groom make offerings of ghee and incense at the fire. The couple are joined by knotting the bride's sari into the scarf of the groom and together they take seven steps around the fire. With each step a blessing is said: the first is for God, the others might be for strength, prosperity, happiness, children, long life, for support and for perfect union. The bride and groom then pray that they will be of one heart and one mind in their love. They then feed each other a mouthful of cake or sweet. A mark of red kumkum and sandalwood paste is put on their foreheads and they are showered with petals and rice grains to wish them happiness and peace.

ASSIGNMENTS

- Some of the things at the Hindu wedding are religious some are just custom or tradition. With a partner decide which are which and list them in two columns. Discuss the meaning of each item.

- Imagine you are the bride's younger brother or sister. Write a letter to a friend about the wedding. Explain what happens and what it all means. Say what you think of the ceremony and whether you would want the same if you marry.

A Hindu wedding in London

RITES OF PASSAGE

CREMATION

● Look at the photo. In what ways is this ceremony different from funerals carried out in our society? What does it tell us about different attitudes to death in Britain and in India? Discuss.

When a Hindu dies the body is cremated. It is believed that during cremation the soul is released and rises to the heavens before it is rekindled in a new life. In India the funeral pyre is out in the open. In Britain the local crematorium carries out the cremation but a Hindu priest will be invited to lead the prayers and recite sacred mantras from the Vedas.

● The god of fire in the Vedas is Agni. He is present on many special occasions and communicates between heaven and earth. List the properties of fire. Discuss the meaning fire might have at a Hindu cremation.

Cremation in India

After the body is washed and anointed with incense it is wrapped in a cloth. It is laid on the funeral pyre. This is built with wood. Sandalwood is added to burn sweetly. The body is covered with more wood and the eldest son of the family sets the fire alight. Into the flames he pours offerings of ghee and sprinkles incense. A priest recites prayers and makes offerings to the god of fire and other deities. The mourners watch and stay until the fire dies down. Everyone prays for the departed:

> After death may the sun absorb your power of sight,
> The breath of the winds carry your soul.
> May you enter the shining levels as your karma permits.
> May all that is water return to the oceans
> And your body return to the soil and be one with the earth.

Taking care of the ashes

Later the ashes are collected and the eldest son in the family takes them to scatter in the river Ganges. It is believed that the waters are so sacred that previous karma is washed away. The widow or widower will wear white after the death of their spouse, which is a sign of mourning. Usually the close family observes twelve days of mourning. However, it is believed to be unwise to show too much grief, for the soul is only continuing on its journey towards moksha, which is the goal of all Hindus.

A cremation pyre

RITES OF PASSAGE   33

ASSIGNMENTS

● Imagine you are a relative at a Hindu cremation in India. Write a letter to a friend in England to tell them what happened at the cremation. Explain the meaning of the ceremony for you. (You may need to research further in other books on Hinduism.)

● Describe two of the Hindu samskaras. Explain the beliefs expressed through these rituals and say how they help Hindus to understand human life. Do you think such rites of passage are important for helping people find meaning and purpose in their lives? Give your own thoughts.

CELEBRATIONS

SHIVA RATRI

Shiva, Vishnu the preserver, and **Brahma** the creator are sometimes called the **Trimurti** because they represent three main aspects of God. Many Hindus worship Shiva as the highest form of God. With his drum and dance he keeps the heartbeat of the universe. Its life is in his hand and by his hand all things will eventually be destroyed. He measures out each life span and knows the hour of each person's death.

- Look at the photo with a partner and think about these questions: What is the meaning of his dance? What can the circle and the flames be symbols for? Shiva stamps on a dwarf, it represents something inside us. What might this be? One of his hands offers protection. Which one? The lifted foot and outstretched hand offer release. Can you suggest what from?

Lord of life and death

Shiva is also Lord of reproduction and is often represented by a smooth phallic-shaped stone or **lingam**. He has the power to destroy all life and to re-create all life. Sometimes he appears as an ascetic (someone who has renounced luxury) deep in meditation, his body smeared with ash and his hair matted (see the photo on page 14). Through prayer and fasting he builds up his unique powers. His image is often guarded by Nandi the bull.

Shiva Nataraj
(the dancing Lord of the universe)

Fasting and feasting

In February or March there is a night dedicated to Lord Shiva. It takes place on the thirteenth day of the darker half of the Hindu month of Magh. Worshippers fast and spend time in devotion at Shiva's shrine. His image is garlanded with flowers. Offerings of milk are poured over the lingam and the priests perform puja. Shiva Ratri is a deeply religious occasion. Some say it celebrates Shiva's wedding to his wife Parvati.

'My mother and I fast at Shiva Ratri to show our love and respect for Lord Shiva. We want to please him and serve him and going without food helps us to learn self-discipline and to be stronger in all our efforts to serve Lord Shiva. At the end of the fast we take food to the temple and everyone celebrates.'

ASSIGNMENTS

- Give up solid food for two meals. Write down the feelings you experienced and what you learnt. List the good and bad things about the fast. Share your thoughts in class.

- Imagine you are a Hindu. Write a diary of the day of the fast and festival. Explain why you fasted and what you hoped to gain from fasting. Explain the meaning of the festival and say what the occasion meant for you and your family.

KEY W●R●S

Brahma   Trimurti   lingam

36 CELEBRATIONS

SPRING FESTIVALS

CELEBRATIONS

Holi

● Look at the pictures of Holi in India today and in the past. List clues that tell you about the time, place and character of the festival. What do these things say about Hinduism?

A well-loved story told at Holi is about a tyrant called Hiranyakashipu.

> King Hiranyakashipu demanded that everyone should worship him, but his son Prahlad would worship only Vishnu. The king tried to force his son to bow down to him. Eventually he made his daughter, Holika, carry Prahlad into the flames of a furnace. She had been promised a gift from the gods that 'she alone would not be destroyed by fire'. But, since she was not alone, she was destroyed. Miraculously the boy lived. Lord Vishnu himself appeared and destroyed the tyrant. Prahlad was crowned and the kingdom rejoiced.

At Holi, bonfires are lit to celebrate the story of good conquering evil. This custom is kept among Hindus living in Britain. Puja is performed at the fire with offerings of rice, ghee and incense. Sometimes coconuts are roasted on the fire. The old custom of squirting everyone with coloured water is still done in India but not here.

Many stories at Holi focus on Krishna as a young cowherd who enchanted milkmaids with the music of his flute. Songs and dances tell of the love between Krishna and his lover Radha. The total self-surrender of Radha to her lord is a symbol of the surrender of the human soul to God. Festivals are an opportunity for people to surrender themselves in devotion to God. They are also important for bringing people together and keeping alive the culture and traditions of the community.

Rama's birthday

In March or April, on the ninth day of the darker half of the Hindu month of Chaitra, Hindus celebrate the birth of Rama. Rama is the seventh avatar of Lord Vishnu. In India the story of Rama is acted out in a series of plays. In Britain there are celebrations at the temple and sometimes a cradle is built and decorated with sweet flowers. At noon, when Rama was born, images of Rama are rocked in the cradle and puja is performed and people bring offerings.

ASSIGNMENTS

● Find out more about these festivals and the stories about Prahlad, Krishna and Rama. Tape record yourself telling one of these stories.

● Imagine you are a Hindu in Britain. Write an article for an Indian magazine about the ways in which Holi and the birthday of Rama are celebrated here. Explain how and why the celebrations in Britain are different. (Remember that spring is colder here than in India.) Say how such occasions are especially important for the Hindu community in Britain.

JANAMASHTAMI

Lord Vishnu takes on different forms. When the powers of evil threaten the world, Hindus believe he is born on earth to preserve humankind. On one of these occasions Vishnu appeared as Lord Krishna. Hindus celebrate the birth of Krishna in summer at the festival of Janamashtami. It falls on the eighth day of the darker half of the month of Shrawan.

● Look at the photo. List the signs that tell you it is a Hindu festival.

Krishna

The story of the birth of Krishna is set at a time when people lived in fear under the evil king Kamsa.

> Kamsa had been warned that his sister would give birth to a son who would destroy him. So the evil Kamsa had each of her children killed at birth. When the eighth child was due he put his sister in a dungeon. The child, Krishna, was born at midnight. His father hid the baby in a basket and slipped past the guards into the stormy night. He had to cross the flooded river Yamuna but it seemed impossible until one of the baby's feet dangled into the waters. The waves retreated and Krishna's father crossed safely. He left the baby beside a farmer's wife while she slept. The farmer and his wife raised the child as their own and, when Krishna grew up, he destroyed Kamsa. The people rejoiced and crowned him as king.

● In pairs discuss the meaning of the story. What does it tell us about Krishna and how Hindus see him?

The God of love

The stories of Krishna tell of his love for his fellow people. He mixed with men and women of all walks of life. He drew people to him with the music of his flute. Krishna's birthday reminds Hindus that God's spirit can be kindled in everyone. Bhajans, or hymns, are sung and stories of his life are told in music and dance and it is a time of great celebration:

> 'At Janamashtami there is an Arti service at the temple. We put garlands of flowers on the images of Krishna and Radha. My sister and I wear new clothes which our parents give us and we get sweets or presents from our grandparents. We have a special meal with all our family and friends and everyone is happy.'

CELEBRATIONS 39

ASSIGNMENTS

- Design a poster to advertise the Janamashtami festivities at the temple, explaining the meaning of the festival and inviting people to come.

Celebrating the birthday of Krishna at a temple. Worshippers rock the image of Krishna in a cradle which has been richly decorated with fruit and flowers

- Find out more about Krishna then make up a conversation between a Hindu priest and a non-Hindu interested in the shrine of Krishna. First think about the questions the non-Hindu might ask. Then write the answers the priest would give, remembering how very important Krishna is for Hindus as God in human form. Act out your conversation with a partner.

NAVA RATRI

The feminine aspect of God in Hinduism is called **Shakti**, meaning cosmic energy, in other words the energy that makes the universe burst with life. Many Hindus worship God as Supreme Mother:

> Om Pareshakti, 'Mother Supreme',
> The power behind all that is and moves.
> The little insect or reptile, bird or beast,
> Man or woman, all these are your children,
> You love them, protect them and care for them.
> The grass, shrubs and trees are all yours.
> You spread your wings to discipline the sun, the moon, stars and planets.
> The four elements – you control them too.
> Your power is bewildering:
> How great are you and how small am I.

● What picture of God comes across in this hymn? Discuss the powers and qualities of this female form of the deity. Draw a figure that represents this. Think carefully about the colours and shapes you use. Write an explanation of your figure.

Nine nights

Nava Ratri means 'nine nights'. It is a festival dedicated to the goddess. The tenth day of the festival is the highpoint, and is known as Dussehra. In India the festival falls in autumn during the light half of the Hindu month of Ashwin. Nava Ratri is celebrated with puja at the shrine of the goddess and with traditional Indian dance.

● With a partner list the qualities and skills a good mother possesses. Discuss which of these might be useful for talking about God. Suggest arguments to show that recognising a female side to God's nature could be helpful. Discuss this in class. Write up a debate showing the different points of view.

Durga puja

In Bengal Nava Ratri is called Durga Puja. **Durga** is their name for the mother goddess. Like all good mothers Durga is protective, she drives away evil. The popular scriptures called the Puranas tell of Durga killing the buffalo demon who threatened heaven and earth. A large clay image of Durga is built during the festival and lavished with flowers and offerings. At the end of the celebrations the image is plunged into the river.

● What happens when you put unfired clay into water? What might the ritual of plunging the image into the river mean? Discuss the importance of this in class and write up your own explanation.

CELEBRATIONS 41

ASSIGNMENTS

● Find out about Durga, Kali, Parvati and Nava Ratri and make illustrated notes.

● In pairs list some of the difficulties you have with the Hindu idea of God. Make another list of the things which you think are helpful about the Hindu approach to God. Share your thoughts with a partner and then write up your views.

KEY WORDS

Shakti   Durga

Durga Puja in India

DIWALI

The word 'Diwali' comes from the name of the ghee lamp called a **diya**, which means lines of lights.

- Read the poem below. Draw out all the information you can about the festival, the beliefs associated with it and the meaning of the celebration for Hindus.

> Wonderful, wonderful festival of lights
> I wish it was Diwali every day every night
> Oh welcome Lakshmi goddess of wealth and light
> Come bless this house and fill our hearts with delight
> We have swept our house, made it shiny tonight
> Our doorstep, back garden, every window every room is alight
> The diyas are twinkling so brightly tonight
> To welcome you here on this moonless night ...
> Oh what a glorious welcome awaits you on this dark dark night
> The puja is done and I kiss my mum and dad goodnight
> The candles by the way are going to glow in the dark all night
> Tread lightly and swiftly, O goddess of light
> I know you have a million trillion houses to visit tonight
> But please, oh please don't miss my house tonight....

Mixing religion and business

The festival of Diwali marks the new business year. Businesses close their accounts. They open up new books and perform puja in honour of the goddess **Lakshmi**.

- Could offering a business to God influence the way a business is run? With a friend sketch out a conversation in which one business person tries to persuade another to join them in Lakshmi puja because they think it is important to offer one's livelihood to God.

Good conquering evil

Diwali is celebrated in different ways in different Hindu communities. Lakshmi is always welcomed with lights at Diwali. Images of the goddess are decorated and presented with offerings. Some Hindus celebrate the coronation of Rama and Sita. Others remember Krishna conquering the demon Narakaasura. For many Hindus Diwali is New Year. Husbands and wives renew their vows and children make new year's resolutions and wear new clothes. Families celebrate with festive food and presents. Festivals draw the community together. Old quarrels are forgiven and hopes for a better future are raised. People try to make a new effort to serve God in their daily lives.

CELEBRATIONS 43

ASSIGNMENTS

● Write a booklet for Hindu children about Diwali and one other Hindu festival. Say how they are celebrated and explain the meaning behind them. Use other books to help you. Explain also why it is important for Hindu children to remember the teachings as well as enjoy the fun.

KEY WORDS

diya   Lakshmi

Lakshmi Puja at Diwali in Britain. The new accounts are opened and given the blessing of the goddess

PILGRIMAGE

AN ACT OF DEVOTION

- Describe a special place – somewhere you want to return to or somewhere you have longed to visit or just a place you will always remember. Describe your feelings and experiences on this visit. Say why it is a special place to you.

For Hindus pilgrimage is an act of devotion or service to God. It often involves great personal sacrifice.

> 'I wanted to make a pilgrimage to the Himalayas and of course to Varanasi to worship Lord Shiva. The fare was quite expensive so we had to save up. Varanasi is on the river Ganges. We bathed in its sacred waters and prayed to Shiva. When we were there we visited the temples and shrines dedicated to Shiva. We hope the pilgrimage will bring us merit in future lives so that we will come closer to attaining moksha.'

Places of pilgrimage

In India there are many places of pilgrimage. The most well known is Benares, also called Varanasi or Kashi. This is on the river Ganges in northern India. Many Hindus also visit Badrinath, north-east of Delhi, high up in the Himalayas. Pilgrimage takes the worshipper out of everyday existence and helps them to see life afresh.

Pilgrims at Badrinath Temple in the Himalayas

Pilgrimage in the scriptures

Devotees of Krishna may go on pilgrimage to Kurukshetra. In the Vamana Purana scriptures it says:

> A man who goes there filled with faith and who bathes in the great pool ... wins whatever his heart desires; of this there is no doubt. A man should practise self-control, circumambulate the lake, seek forgiveness again and again and ... offer flowers and incense and food to the god and recite the following: 'By your grace ... I shall make a pilgrimage to whatever sacred fords, forests and rivers there may be. Make my way ever clear.'

- List the information given in the quotations on:
  a) the purpose of pilgrimage
  b) the activities carried out on a pilgrimage.

ASSIGNMENTS

- Find out about places of pilgrimage in India. Draw a map of India showing six places and write a few sentences on each.

- Imagine you are one of the pilgrims in the photo. Draw and write a postcard back home. You may want to:
  a) express your excitement about being in the Himalayas
  b) describe the temple or shrine you have visited
  c) mention the other people sharing your experiences on the prilgrimage
  d) say why you are on pilgrimage.

THE RIVER GANGES

- Look at the photo of pilgrims at the Ganges. List the different expressions of worship that you can identify. What does this tell you about pilgrimage?

The Ganges is sometimes called 'Mother Ganga' as if it were a goddess. The river is especially associated with the Lord Shiva. There is a story behind this:

> Ganga, the river goddess, was reluctant to come down to earth because her immense power would be too destructive. She only agreed to come when Shiva, who lives in the Himalayas, agreed to tie her down by using the locks of his hair. (The locks are the forests and, too late, Indian planners are rediscovering the truth in the legend.)

- Read this story with a partner and discuss its meaning. Write down words which come to mind which might be used to describe the meaning of the river Ganges for Hindus. Use them to write a prayer or poem about 'Mother Ganga'.

Many Hindus choose to visit the Ganges before they die to bathe in the sacred waters. They believe it washes away the karma that binds the soul to earthly existence. Worshippers stand in the waters to bathe, to pray, to make offerings of flowers and fruit, and water is lifted up in the hands as an offering to the sun.

The eldest son of a family may travel to the Ganges with the ashes of a parent or relative to scatter them on the waters. There are many places along the banks of the river where cremations are carried out. Hindus believe that if the ashes are strewn into the Ganges the soul will be freed from the karma that hinders its progress to moksha. Some Hindu families keep a bottle of water from the Ganges to anoint the dying in the belief that this will carry the same blessing.

ASSIGNMENTS

- Find out more about the city of Varanasi and the river Ganges.
- Imagine you are a Hindu keeping a diary on your pilgrimage. Write it up in three sections (use some other books to help you):
  a) when you are looking ahead to the trip – write about your hopes and fears
  b) on the journey itself – describe the trip and the visits you make
  c) on your return home – describe your thoughts and memories and say what it all meant to you.
- Some pilgrims believe that pilgrimage brings them spiritual merit. What do *you* think the advantages of pilgrimage are? Make a list of these and compare them with a partner's.

The river Ganges at Varanasi

GURU AS GOD

Hindus believe that God can take on a physical body and visit the earth. The physical form of God is called an incarnation or avatar. Remember, the word avatar means 'down-coming'. Krishna is an avatar of Vishnu. In the Bhagavad Gita he says:

> Whenever the law of righteousness [dharma]
> Withers away, and lawlessness
> Raises its head
> Then do I generate myself on earth.
> For the protection of the good,
> For the destruction of evildoers,
> For the setting up of righteousness,
> I come into being, age after age.
>
> [Bhagavad Gita IV, 7–8]

Enlightened beings

Many Hindus follow a **guru** or spiritual teacher, believing him to be the incarnation of God in this age. The guru Sri Sai Baba of Shirdi is renowned for his tolerance and respect for all religions and his love for his followers. Many of his devotees go on pilgrimage to hear his teachings and to visit the shrine dedicated to him. Here is the account of a pilgrim from England:

> 'The way of worship there was different. Everyone got up very early in the morning, had their baths and went to the temple. We did not have any breakfast. Here we saw a marble statue of Sai Baba which was decorated with flowers. Incense sticks were burning and the atmosphere was electric. We were allowed to take part in the worship as a family which was different from any other temple. We really felt very close to Sai Baba. It may be because he looked like an ordinary human being, who had appeared from nowhere but helped all people. We could relate to him. He was not like other gods who were just symbols. There were no inhibitions or obstructions in observing Sai Baba's religion. After the worship and receiving the parshad we really felt fulfilled. We toured around the village, saw a little shrine where he had worshipped, the tree under which he appeared and felt the true atmosphere.'

- Hindus believe that God can reveal himself in human form. What quality of life and what qualities of character would you look for in such a person?
- Look at the photo of the guru and his devotees. What do the actions of the worshippers tell you about their feelings for the guru and the meaning of this pilgrimage for them?

ASSIGNMENTS

● Read again the description of the pilgrimage opposite. With a partner write down all the ways in which the guru is treated like a god. The idea of God becoming a man is unacceptable to some people. Does it make God easier to understand or is it hard to accept? Discuss this in pairs and then in class and write up the ideas in an essay.

KEY WORDS

guru

50 PILGRIMAGE

PERSONAL PILGRIMAGE

PILGRIMAGE

Sometimes a pilgrimage fulfils a personal promise or vow to God. For example a mother whose child is very ill may pray to the goddess Durga to cure her baby. When her child recovers she may feel that the best way to say thank you is to go on a pilgrimage to Ambaji where there are shrines to the mother goddess. In this way her pilgrimage is a personal act of thanksgiving and an expression of faith.

Acts of devotion

During a pilgrimage worshippers may take part in a number of activities, some more clearly religious than others. Many of the places of pilgrimage are believed to be particularly sacred because of their association with a god or goddess. Attending Arti or puja at the shrine or temple of the god may be the highlight of the journey. Catching a glimpse of the deity at the climax of the service, when the presence of the god is most felt, is called **darshan**.

> 'Durga's shrine was right at the centre, surrounded by devotees all eager to move forward and see the goddess herself. There was so much noise and excitement... I was excited, and scared. When I saw her image it was even more of a shock. Even now it feels that at that moment she was also seeing me.'

Pilgrims at Kedarnath
in the Himalayas

People may make special vows while on a pilgrimage involving fasting or circumambulation (making a circuit) of the shrine a number of times. Sometimes the pilgrimage involves ritual washing such as bathing in the river Ganges.

Sharing the same journey

Meeting people who share the same hopes and beliefs is another aspect of pilgrimage. It might mean sharing the same journey and meeting the difficulties together, eating together and coming together for worship. Places of pilgrimage are often of historical interest and so sightseeing may play a part in the overall plan too. Buying souvenirs and gifts to take back to friends and family is also an entertaining side to the trip.

- Why do you think pilgrims want to buy things to take back with them? What will they take back that cannot be bought? Discuss this with a partner and share your ideas in class.

ASSIGNMENTS

- Some people say that life is a pilgrimage. With a partner discuss what you think is meant by this and discuss ways in which your own life is like a journey. On your own, design a picture which expresses this and write a brief explanation underneath.

KEY WORDS

darshan

VALUES

THE WORLD

- What are the usual aims most people have in life? List them. With a partner discuss which of these aims you think are important.

The final aim of every Hindu is to attain moksha. However, there are also important aims for life in this world. There are teachings governing the three pursuits of kama or pleasure, artha which is wealth or property, and dharma or righteousness. In all these pursuits Hindus should show self-discipline and reverence for Brahman in all things.

- What does it mean when someone is self-disciplined? How would it show in:
  a) their eating habits
  b) their attitude to luxuries
  c) their daily routine e.g. work, relaxation
  d) their attitude to using the world's resources?

Maya

The world is 'maya' according to Hinduism. **Maya** has two meanings. Firstly it means creative power. The world can be seen as the outward expression of God's creative power. Maya also means appearance or illusion. In this sense the world is not real in the way that God is real. It has no independent reality. The world and everything in it can be seen as like a dream because it is only temporary and cannot last. Only Brahman is eternal.

- Is the world constantly changing? Does anything in it last for ever? What does this tell us about choosing our aims in life?

The god Brahma

The creative powers of God are represented in the deity Brahma. (Not to be confused with Brahman.) Hindu teachings say that there are times when the universe comes into being and times when it dissolves back into nothingness. In between being dissolved and being re-created is what is called the sleep of Vishnu. It is captured in this myth:

> When there were no heavens and no earth only the ocean of eternity, Lord Vishnu slept, rocked on the waves in the coils of a mighty serpent. A sound stirred the depths Ommmmmmm and awoke Lord Vishnu. Brahma appeared in the petals of a lotus flower and Vishnu commanded him to create the universe. Brahma divided the lotus flower into three to make the heavens, the earth and the skies. He filled the earth with plants and gave them feeling. Then he created insects, animals and birds. To these he gave the five senses. Lastly he created humankind.

ASSIGNMENTS

● Write down three ways in which your view of the world and life is different from the Hindu world-view. Then write down the things they have in common. With a friend look at your different views and discuss them. Say what you find attractive about the Hindu world-view and what things you find difficult.

KEY WORDS

maya

Vishnu, and the birth of Brahma in a lotus flower

VALUES

NON-VIOLENCE

Reverence for life

The word **ahimsa** is important in Hinduism. It is often translated as non-violence but it really means more than pacifism or non-violence. It is an attitude of love and humility towards all other beings. It springs from the respect for all life that is at the heart of the Hindu faith. Hindus believe that Brahman is in all things, and that animals as well as people have souls. Many Hindus are vegetarian for this reason.

This reverence for life goes back to the earliest scriptures. In the Vedas the hymn to the Breath of Life speaks of the same life force being in all things:

> The Breath of Life takes living creatures as its garment.
>
> [Atharva Veda XI, iv, 10]

The belief in the sacredness of life can also be seen in the reverence for the cow in India. The cow provides milk for food and is a symbol of the fruitfulness of life. Gandhi said:

> 'Cow protection to me is one of the most wonderful things in all human evolution; for it takes the human being beyond his species. Man through the cow is enjoined to realise his identity with all that lives.... Cow protection is the gift of Hinduism to the world.'

Hindus believe that harmful actions in this life will lead to more harm in the future because of the law of karma. Those who deal out violence in this life will build up bad karma. So most Hindus try to avoid causing any sort of harm in the world.

- What might be the attitude of many devout Hindus to:
  a) testing products on animals
  b) eating beef
  c) foxhunting
  d) pollution, e.g. widespread use of insecticides?
  Suggest reasons for these attitudes.

- Look back at the sections on reincarnation and birth ceremonies, pages 16–17 and 24–5. In the light of the teaching of ahimsa, what do you think will be the attitude of many devout Hindus on the issue of abortion? Discuss the different possible interpretations in class.

ASSIGNMENTS

- Find out more about Gandhi and his reverence for life. Write a report on Gandhi's views concerning non-violence. Give examples from his life to show his attitude put into practice. Say what your own attitude is on this issue. Explain the ways in which you agree with Gandhi and the things with which you may not agree.

KEY WORDS

ahimsa

56 VALUES

WAR AND PEACE

VALUES

What the scriptures say

There are two types of Hindu scripture. The oldest are the **srti** meaning 'revealed', these include the Vedas and Upanishads. There are other scriptures called **smrti** meaning 'remembered'. These contain the stories such as the Ramayana, the Puranas and the **Mahabharata**. The Mahabharata is about a war between the Pandava brothers and their evil cousins the Kauravas. Driven by jealousy, the Kauravas robbed the Pandavas of their kingdom. The Pandavas tried every possible peaceful means to restore the land to their people. However, all efforts to come to a just and peaceful arrangement failed. In the end they had to go to war.

The leader of the Pandavas was Arjuna. His charioteer was Krishna. When the battle lines were drawn up, Arjuna became panic-stricken and put down his arms. He said he could not fight. He argued it must be wrong to kill one's own kith and kin and was horrified at the chaos that would result from war. Krishna's reply is found in the Bhagavad Gita, which is a part of the Mahabharata.

- Look at the photo of the Bhagavad Gita. What does this tell you about the way in which Hindus regard the words of Krishna? Discuss this with a partner.

The Bhagavad Gita in a shrine

The teaching of the Bhagavad Gita

Krishna tells Arjuna that to fight for justice and truth is to fulfil the law of God. He argues from three points: firstly it is Arjuna's dharma as a prince and soldier to fight for the good of his people. Secondly he can only cause the death of men's bodies, he cannot hurt their souls. Lastly, he is not fighting for personal gain. That would be wrong. He must fight to the best of his ability without seeking gain or glory and without hatred or bitterness. With these words Krishna persuades Arjuna to fight and the Pandavas restored their kingdom for their people.

- The original caste system set out in the scriptures ensured that the community had a trained army so that ordinary people would not be involved in battle. If Hindus based their views on the scriptures how would they respond to:
  a) the bombing of towns and villages
  b) the use of nuclear weapons
  c) the use of war to gain more land?
  Discuss your answers with a partner.

ASSIGNMENTS

- Is it sometimes right to fight? If so, when? Work in groups on a class debate. Take Krishna's arguments on the one side, and the arguments of Arjuna on the other. Prepare the arguments carefully. Look at the situation in the story and Krishna's sermon. You may want to use other books to help you. Debate the issue in class and write up the arguments as you see them and give your conclusions.

KEY WORDS

srti   smrti   Mahabharata

LOVE AND MARRIAGE

● Look at the ideas below. Say which ones you think best describe what getting married is about, then write your own:

The perfect conclusion to a perfect romance.
Making a contract to live together and share everything.
Setting up a home together with a view to a family.
A way of satisfying physical needs and avoiding loneliness.

● Compare your ideas with the Hindu idea of marriage below:

> Marriage, according to Hindu scriptures, represents the second stage in the pilgrimage of life. Hindu marriage is a sacrament based on the ideal of a holy bond of union for spiritual development, mutual love and companionship in the service of God, mankind and the universe at large.
>
> [The Gujurati Centre Handbook, Preston]

Assisted marriage

Hindu parents believe they would be failing in their love and duty to their son or daughter if they did not try to find a suitable marriage partner for them. If the son or daughter is not happy with the parents' choice they can say they would rather wait until someone more suitable is found. Usually the families are already known to one another. Here are the thoughts of a Hindu teenage girl on assisted marriage today:

> 'I know all my friends at school will choose who they marry but I want my parents to find someone they know will be right for me. It is such a big decision. I trust my parents and I know I will not be forced into something I'm not happy with.'

● With a friend list the factors you think a good parent will take into account in looking for a partner for their daughter.

Hindus prefer their sons and daughters not to get involved with young people of the opposite sex before they have finished their studies. One ashrama, or stage in life, must be completed faithfully before the next is entered into.

● Hindus can get divorced but this is rare. Why do you think this is? Discuss the possible reasons in class.

ASSIGNMENTS

● Read again the words of the Hindu girl about marriage. With a friend write questions you would like to ask her. List the similarities and the differences between your idea of marriage and hers. What problems do you think the girl might encounter or need to think carefully about? What are the risks with *your* outlook on love and marriage? Discuss the arguments in favour of each point of view.

A Hindu wedding in India

60 VALUES

COMMUNITY SERVICE

VALUES

● Look at this timetable for a Hindu community centre. Working in pairs list the activities under three headings: 'Service to Others', 'Worship' and 'The Path to Moksha'. Discuss your lists.

Hindu community and cultural centre

Day/Time	Group/Club	Activity/Worship
Monday		
10–12	Senior Citizens	Puja, coffee, cards
1.30–2	Play Group	Games and toys
6 pm	General	Arti service
Tuesday		
10–12	Young Mothers	Puja, coffee, chat
12.30–2	Senior Citizens	Lunch
3.30–5	After School Club	Story reading
6 pm	General	Puja and Arti
Wednesday		
10–12	Senior Citizens	Meditation and lunch
2–3	Play Group	Toys and stories
6–8 pm	Youth Club	Meditation class
Thursday		
10–12.30	Young Mothers	Coffee, speaker
3.30–5	After School Club	Playtime
6 pm	General	Arti
Friday		
10 am	Senior Citizens	Recital of B'Gita
6 pm	General	Arti
7.30–10	Youth Club	Games, coffee, chat
Saturday		
9–11	Hindu and Urdu	Classes 1 and 2
11–12.30	Punjabi	Classes 1 and 2
2–4	General	Meditation
4–5	Bengali	Classes 1 and 2
6–8.30 pm	General	Arti service
Sunday		
10	General	Arti
2–4	Indian Cultural Group	Indian music
6 pm	General	Arti service
8 pm	General	Community meal

NOTICE: Please bring your unwanted clothes, toys and household items, or sweets and cakes for the bring-and-buy sale next week in aid of the 'New Wing for Cancer Care' at the hospital.

A Hindu community playgroup in London

The teachings of the scriptures

The Hindu scriptures point to a way of life which has three main aims: to love and worship God, to live true to one's dharma and in service of others, to work towards release from this earthly existence.

● Look through the references to the different Hindu scriptures mentioned in this book. List them under 'Smrti' and 'Srti'. Beside each one say what it contains or indicate some aspects of its teaching.

In India there are schools, hospitals and centres set up by Hindu charities. The same spirit of community service can be seen in Hindu temples in this country. Visitors are always welcomed with warm hospitality, for the scriptures say that you should treat three groups of people like gods: your parents, your teacher and the stranger or guest who comes to visit.

ASSIGNMENTS

● Imagine you live in the town where the Hindu community run a programme like the one opposite. Write a letter to a local newspaper describing the work of the Hindu centre. Comment on the value of its work in the community.

● Some Hindu mandirs have had to keep their doors shut due to vandalism. Imagine you belong to the committee of the mandir. You do not want relations with the outside community to be soured by this sort of thing. In a group decide on a policy for the mandir in which it tries to create good relations with the local community, e.g. through contact with local schools etc. Draw up a year's programme of activities. Say what you aim to achieve by your efforts. Compare and share your ideas in class.

Glossary

ahimsa Non-violence, not harming, respect for life
Arti Offering of light with five-flame lamp
ashrama Stage of life
atman Personal soul or spirit
avatar 'Down-coming' – incarnation
Bhagavad Gita 'Song of the Lord' – most well-loved scripture, from 4th to 2nd centuries BCE, in the Mahabharata
bhajan Devotional hymn or song
bhakti yoga Way of love leading to moksha; 'bhakti' means devotion to God, love
Brahma Hindu Lord of creation (not to be confused with Brahman); one of the three main aspects of God
brahma charya First stage of life – student
Brahman Hindu Supreme Spirit, Ultimate Reality, God
brahmin Priest, one of the four varnas – the priestly class
darshan Sight or glimpse of a deity at a sacred shrine or place of pilgrimage
dharma What is right, duty, universal law, religion is perhaps the best translation
diya Ghee lamp with a number of flames
Durga Hindu mother goddess in her most popular form
Gayatri Mantra Sacred prayer to the god of the sun – Savitri, in the Vedas
grihastha Second stage of life – householder
guru Spiritual teacher
Havan Fire ritual used in many ceremonies
jati Kinship group often related to work or a profession, also called 'caste'
jnana yoga Way of knowledge leading to moksha; 'jnana' means knowledge
karma Actions, law of cause and effect
karma yoga Way of unselfish action leading to moksha
Krishna Avatar of Vishnu, whose teachings are given in the Bhagavad Gita
kshatriya One of the four varnas – the warrior and princely class
Lakshmi Hindu goddess of wealth and light
lingam Phallic symbol representing Lord Shiva and the power to create life
Mahabharata One of the smrti or 'remembered' scriptures, an epic dating from about 9th century BCE
mandir Hindu temple
mantra Sacred teaching, prayer or chant usually from the scriptures, e.g. OM, or the name of the god
maya Illusion, appearance, creative power
moksha Release or liberation from the eternal cycle of karma and samsara
OM Sacred sound and symbol representing eternal truth, used in meditation
panchamrit Mixture of yogurt, honey, milk, ghee and sugar, used to bathe a deity
parshad Blessed food offered at a shrine
puja Devotion through offerings at a shrine
Rama Avator of Vishnu, whose story is told in the Ramayana
samsara The eternal cycle of the soul through birth, life, death and rebirth
samskar A sacred ritual to mark the start of a new stage in life
Sanatandharma The Hindu's own word for their faith, meaning 'eternal dharma'
sannyasin Last stage of life, also a spiritual seeker and world renouncer
Shakti Female aspect of God, cosmic energy
Shiva One of the three main aspects of God, in particular the power of destruction
shudra One of the four varnas – the servant class
smrti (or smirti) 'Remembered' scriptures
srti (or shruti) 'Revealed' scriptures (including Vedas and Upanishads)
Trimurti Brahma, Vishnu and Shiva – the three main aspects of God
Upanayam (Sacred Thread Ceremony) Ritual marking the first stage in life
Upanishads 'Sit down near' scriptures at the end of the Vedas, containing teachings of the gurus to their students from the srti or revealed texts
vaishya One of the four varnas – the business class
vanprasthashram Third stage of life – turning to spiritual well-being
varna Class in ancient Hindu society
Vedas Srti or 'revealed' scriptures, dating from 1500 BCE, the most sacred of Hindu texts
Vishnu One of the three main aspects of God, the Preserver, appearing as Rama and Krishna
yantra (mandala) Design or pattern used for focusing the mind in meditation

Index

Agni 32
ahimsa 54
Amba 15
Arjuna 57
artha 52
Arti 9, 12–13, 38, 51, 61
ashrama 26–7, 58
atman 16
avatar 23, 48
Benares *see* Varanasi
Bhagavad Gita 4, 16, 48, 57, 61
bhajans 6, 12, 38
bhakti yoga 19
Brahma 35, 52–3
brahma charya 26–7
Brahman 4, 10–11, 15, 16, 19, 52, 54
brahmin 20–1, 26
dharma 20, 22–3, 26–7, 48, 52, 57, 61
Diwali 42–3
Durga 15, 40–1, 51
Dussehra 40
Gandhi, Mahatma 54
Ganges 32, 45, 46–7, 51
Gayatri Mantra 9, 24–5, 29
grihastha 26–7
gunas 19
guru 17, 29, 48–9
Havan 24, 31
Hinduism 4 (*see also* Sanatandharma)
Holi 36–7
Janamashtami 38–9
jati 20
jnana yoga 19
Kali 15
kama 52
karma 16–17, 19, 32, 46, 54
karma yoga 19
Krishna 4–5, 15, 19, 37, 38–9, 42, 45, 48, 57

kshatriya 20, 26
Lakshmi 42–3
lingam 35
Mahabharata 56–7
mandir 12
mantras 6, 9, 11, 24–5, 29
marriage 30–1, 58–9
maya 18–19, 52
meditation 10–11, 19, 27, 29, 61
moksha 19, 27, 32, 45, 46, 52
Nava Ratri 40–1
OM 11, 52–3
parshad 9, 12
puja 9, 12, 35, 37, 40, 42–3, 51, 61
Puranas 40, 45, 57
Rama 15, 22–3, 37, 42
Ramayana 23, 57
Sacred Thread *see* Upanayam
samsara 16–17, 19
samskar 28–9, 31
Sanatandharma 22–3
sannyasin 10–11, 27
Shakti 40
Shiva 14–15, 34–5, 45, 46
shudra 20
smrti 57
srti 57
Trimurti 35
Upanayam 28–9
Upanishads 10–11, 15, 16, 19, 57
vaishya 20, 26
vanprasthashram 27
Varanasi 45, 46–7
varnas 20–1, 26
Vedas 10, 20, 29, 31, 32, 54, 57
Vishnu 15, 23, 35, 37, 38, 48, 52–3
yantras 10–11
yoga 11

Further reading

Bahree, P. *The Hindu World*. In *Religions of the World* series, Macdonald, 1982

Brown, A., J. Rankin and A. Wood. *Religions*, Longman, 1988

Collinson, C. and C. Miller. *Milestones: Rites of Passage in a Multi-Faith Community*, Edward Arnold, 1984

Gavin, J. *The Hindu World*. In *Stories from Religions of the World* series, Macdonald, 1986

Jackson, R. *Hinduism*. In *Religions through Festivals*, Longman, 1989

Kanitkar, V.P. (Hemant). *Hindu Festivals and Sacraments*, V.P. Kanitkar, 1984 (available from: V.P. Kanitkar, 83 Bulwer Road, New Barnet, Herts EN5 5EU)

——*Hinduism*. In *Religions of the World* series, Wayland, 1986

Mitter, S. *Hindu Festivals*, Wayland, 1985

Oldfield, K. *Hindu Gods and Goddesses*, CEM, 1987

Sharma, D. *Hindu Belief and Practice*, Edward Arnold, 1984

Sharpe, E.J. *Thinking about Hinduism*, Lutterworth, 1988

Zaehner, R.C. (ed.) *Hindu Scriptures*, Dent, 1966

Acknowledgements

We are indebted to the following for permission to reproduce copyright material:

J.M. Dent & Sons Ltd for extracts from *Hindu Scriptures* translated by R.C. Zaehner (pub. Everyman's Library, 1966); Shap Working Party for an extract from *Shap Mailing 1983* edited by Mary Hayward; the author, V.P. (Hemant) Kanitkar for extracts from *Hindu Festivals and Sacraments* (Barnet, 1984); the author, Nina Sethi for her poem 'Welcome Diwali Festival of Lights'.

We are unable to trace the copyright holder in a booklet published by an Interfaith Movement in the UK (page 40) and would be grateful for any information which would enable us to do so.

We are grateful to the following for permission to reproduce photographs:

Mohammed Ansar, pages 5, 8, 11, 21, 25, 28, 30, 34, 43, 56, 60; Sally & Richard Greenhill, page 47; Derek Henderson, page 33; Hutchison Library, pages 17, 44 (photo: Dave Brinicombe); Nan Melville, page 18; Kim Naylor, page 50; E. Nesbitt, page 36 *below*; Panos Pictures, page 59 (photo: Bror Karlsson); Ann & Bury Peerless Slide Resources & Picture Library, pages 7, 14, 22, 36 *above*, 41, 53, 55; The Photo Co-op, pages 26–27 (photo: Crispin Hughes); David Richardson, page 39; Peter Sanders, page 49; Tim Smith, page 13; Madhu Khanna: *Yantra the Tantric Symbol of Cosmic Unity*. Publ. Thames & Hudson, page 10.

Cover: Sacred Thread Ceremony. Photo: Mohammed Ansar.

LONGMAN GROUP UK LIMITED
Longman House, Burnt Mill, Harlow,
Essex CM20 2JE, England
and Associated Companies throughout the world.

© Longman Group UK Limited 1991
All rights reserved. No part of this publication may be reproduced, stored in a retrieval system, or transmitted in any form or by any means, electronic, mechanical, photocopying, recording, or otherwise without either the prior written permission of the Publishers or a licence permitting restricted copying issued by the Copyright Licensing Agency Ltd, 90 Tottenham Court Road, London W1P 4HE.

First published 1991
ISBN 0 582 02968 6

Set in 11/14 Garamond
Produced by Longman Group (FE) Ltd
Printed in Hong Kong